# TABLE OF CONTENTS

# TIME WILL TELL

And here I am. I took my leave as soon as I was done. She said that opportunity comes but once and I know what she said. I know it very well but I didn't abide by it. I walked down the road, watching as cars wheeze pass me. I tried to control my emotions from appearing on my face. They say the cold ones are the prettiest, the coolest and the smartest. They hide their talents behind their cold faces and they are well respected, unlike the ones with emotions written on their faces. I turned towards old agric hall. The paint has since faded away leaving a dull cement behind. The school never tried to repaint it. It maybe that they just didn't have enough or maybe, they just weren't bordered.

Releasing a sign, I thought about what my face would look like. Is it as blank as I thought it would actually look or is that wishful thinking? I entered old agric hall and sat on the first seat close to the door. Some of my classmates were around. They were smiling and taking last pics before the semester ends. Kelechi had her phone posed in front of her and smiling; her clique were sitting around her. They had smiles similar to hers and some posed with two fingers close to the phone while others posed with one eye close and others bit their lips. The activity is familiar with me but the circumstances is different.

Today is our last day as students of University of Nigeria, Nsukka, UNN. We wrote our last paper today and everyone's excited because tomorrow, which is a Saturday, is finalist night. We will celebrate four years in the university, four years of assignments, projects, 7am lectures, exams and whatnot. It's going to be a must celebratory of the year. I was looking forward to that day until yesterday or more like, today.

I got ready yesterday and went to the pharmacy building in the night for night reading. I read for two hours and as usual, I took my three-hour nap but unlike usual, I didn't wake up after three hours. I woke up thirty minutes before the exam. I had to rush to the exam hall. I went through all I've read till yesterday but I didn't have enough. It was minute compared to what I was supposed to know and I was already in tears when I answered my name. The exam didn't help either. The questions weren't familiar and I was at a dead end. I wrote based on the words that sounded somewhat familiar and also on what I knew.

At the end, I turned up something but I'm not confident like I was in my previous papers. I left the exam hall and here I am. I sat up when Dinma came into the hall. She smiled when she saw me and said,

"How was it?"

I smiled and said,

"It was okay?"

"Don't worry..." she said, "...I don't know what I wrote either. We will pass by the grace of God."

I scrunched my face and nodded at her. I don't believe her. She was reading when I woke up and she didn't try to wake me. I felt betrayed when I saw her but I didn't say anything. She kept on chattering and trying to get me to take pictures with her. I didn't smile. I just glanced at the phone and focused on the whiteboard plastered on the wall in front of me. At a point, I got fed up, stood up and left the hall. Dinma didn't follow me. I didn't turn back to see the expression on her face. I kept on walking, lost in thought and going wherever my feet led me.

The sun is setting and the sky is getting darker. I looked around and found myself in front of Abuja building. I went in and took the stairs. The hallways were dark and devoid of students as I walked through them. I climbed the fourth stairs and tried to climb the next one but someone must have blocked it. Two palm fronds were placed strategically at the top of the fifth stairs in an X format. A thin white rope was tied around each branch in order to hold them together, standing erect and blocking any intruder that would climb to the top of the building.

I stared at the blockade for a while and turned towards the opening leading to the top of the building. Abuja building is built in a way that there are openings on the walls, wide enough for a person my size can pass through. The starless night sky glared at me. I sat close to the edge of the building and stared at the ground four floors down. If maybe I don't see my results, I won't have to repeat classes, I asked myself. With that thought in mind, I released my hands and fell down. I am scared of death, I thought to myself. Why did I take this decision, I thought as I took that free fall.

Everyone looked under Amarachi's name. She's one of the graduates with a 4.8 GPA. Dinma was angry as she stared at the results. It was a small chance. Just a number as little as 0.1 and she would be on par with her. Even after that little stunt before their last exam, Amarachi still managed to get first class. She should have died, Dinma thought.


At ESUT Teaching Hospital Parklane, Enugu, Ada rushed into the orthopedic and surgical ward with a flask of food. She rushed towards bed number five and started gasping.

"Where is she?" she screamed.

A nurse held her and said,

"Relax. She went out to stretch herself. She's with one of the nurses."


Ada watched as Amarachi came in. Even up till today, she couldn't understand why her daughter would want to commit suicide. It always made her melancholy and confused whenever she remembered how they called her in the middle of the night. She wondered what would have happened if no one had been there or if she had landed on her head. She's thankful for how fast her daughter is recovering. Her daughter came in with the nurse and said,

"Mum, how are you doing?"

## MY ONLY REGRET

Waking up in my grandmother's thatched hut still hurts like yesterday's wound. I blinked up at the mud ceiling and looked towards the unsheltered window. Wind blew into the hut through this openings which is only covered by a handful of palm fronds. I sat up and I could feel my aching back sting with pain as I stretched my arms. The hard bamboo bed I slept on never fails to remind me of my sore back. I don't need a watch to know that it's six am on the dot. I've learnt to wake up with the tides.

Leaving my warm hut, I took the empty calabash situated under a bamboo shed, put a pad on my head that would balance the calabash and went on my way to the stream which is a long way from Mama's compound. This brought back unshed tears from my maiden days before Obi whisked me away to the city.

I met some women coming back from the stream. They woke up earlier than me because they are use to the village. They gave me unconcealed daunting looks and I pretended like I didn't see them. As always, I trekked down to the stream, fetched my water and trekked back up. I did this every morning now not minding my sore back. Looking back, I couldn't help but remember the day Chika and I were walking down to the stream; my last day in the village.

"So, Obi has decided that you are worthy of marriage to him?" she had said.

"Yes," I had said, proud of my newfound confidence, "He has decided to marry me."

"Why? It's not like you are more experience than us or anything." she had said.

"He said that he wanted a virgin." I had said.

"He is lying. Men don't want virgins. They are just a baggage in bed." she had replied while wrinkling her nose like what she had said was disgusting.

I was only sixteen. I didn't know what it meant to be a housewife. No one told me, not even Mama told me what to do. I relied heavily on my friends but I can see how stupid I was. How ignorant that made me. Returning from the stream, I swept the compound, stopping at Mama's hut to greet her. She nodded her head but didn't say anything. The old one has been sick since I arrived from the city. I didn't know about it until I was taken to the village.

Despite the sickness, she still has the strength to yell at me whenever she deems fit. She's like a tornado that won't run with the tide unless disturbed. I dropped the broom under the bamboo shed and sat on a bench, making finishing touches the baskets I will sell in the market. Mama got out of her hut with her raffia fan and headed towards me. I dropped the palm fronds I had in my hand and stared at her.

"Are you daft? Where is my snuff?" she said.

"What..." I tried to ask but she interrupted me.

"I say, where is my snuff? You stole it, you she goat. Your husband married a thief..." she sputtered, her Igbo words merging to one string of words.

"If you knew me when I was younger, I was the pride of *òdeñegú*..." she muttered more words that I rarely paid any attention to.

I stood still, staring at the ground as she kept on talking on and on about the same thing I've heard too many times.

"What are you still doing?" she startled me, her voice sounding unruly like the rest of her.

"Go get me my food, you foolish girl." she shouted.

I scrambled off and ran towards the kitchen. The ashes of yesterday's fire felt cold on my palm but I could fix with a little *èvūvū*. Starting the fire, I put a pot of water on the fire and started peeling the yam. This reminded me the easy way it was to prepare a meal oin Obi's kitchen. We had a gas cooker in a brightly lit kitchen. I didn't have to use *èvūvū* to start the fire. The first time Obi showed me how to use it, I was amazed. It was so easy that I felt like a lazy fool. My friends in Lagos affirmed it but I couldn't use *èvūvū* even if I wanted to. I prepared yam porridge for Mama and took the plate of food to her hut. She tasted it and poured the rest of the porridge in the moth eaten mud floor.

"Why is the food hot?" she screamed, "Why can't I have a decent meal in this house?"

Tears prickled my eyes but I held them in and said,

"Mama, I will get another one."

I had to clean up the mess because she said that am lazy and I couldn't tell my left foot from my right. Mama wasn't always like this. She has always had a temper since I was a small girl but after I returned from the city, she has gotten worst. I took a new plate of porridge to her. This time, I decided to feed her and she didn't complain. It reminded me of all the alone moments I had with Obi.

Even though he never touched me, he insisted that I feed him. At first, it sounded like he was a little child that requires taking care of but I still did it. He always had a smile for me whenever I fed him. I would sit on his lap and spoon feed him and he would laugh after swallowing a morsel.

A resounding slap brought me back to reality. The food is on the floor again and I stared at Mama, tears stinging my eyes.

"Stupid girl, if you don't want to feed me, give me my own food "

I cleaned up the mess amidst tears and got her another plate. The food left in the pot was minimum compared to what I want to eat. But I've lost my appetite after I thought about Obi. I remembered the day I went to Madam Chiegu's house. She invited me and I didn't want to disappoint her. She had a large man over as well as me. The large man gave me an unpleasant look and I didn't like it. I tried to brighten my face and look happy.

Madam Chiegu took me and the man to a room with a large bed covered in a white bedsheet. She left us to get drinks. The man closed the door and locked it. He said that he loves me and have been loving me since the first time he saw me. I knew that this was wrong but I could remember feeling excitement that someone was touching me. Obi never touched me in that way and I wondered why.

I don't remember everything that happened but I could remember that I couldn't walk properly that day. I remember the shame that had befallen me and how the man had laughed at how naive I was. I ran out of that house and into my room. I cried and refused to come out when Obi came back.

Since then, I never smiled nor laughed whenever Obi wanted to have fun with me. He noticed it and asked me what was wrong. I was too scared to tell him and so, I said nothing. A week later, he started acting strange as well. He never laughed nor smiled at me and he always stayed up late; arriving drunk to the house as well. I asked him what was wrong but he ignored me.

A week later, Madam Chiegu was taken away in a police van. I never tried to find out why. I was just happy that she would rot in prison. That same day, Obi came back sober for the first time. He wasn't as happy as I thought he would be if he were sober and I didn't ask. Our home was as silent as a graveyard everyday. I never came out to talk to my so called Lagos friends and neighbors. They never bothered me either.

I carried the already made baskets on my head and headed to the market. I dropped them on the ground under my shed in the market. I sat on a low stool and looked at the people passing by. The market women stood up in their barely tied wrappers shouting to passers-by to buy their wares; how cheap they are and how high quality they are. Most of them stopped to look at this cheap, high quality wares. Some would buy it while others would ignore it. Somepeople stopped to look at my wares as well but I don't care if they bought it or not.

An expensive car passed through the road and packed under a mango tree. The little children crowded it, stopping the driver from opening the door.

"That is Aja, the Chief's son. He has come back from oyinbo land." one of the market women said.

"They say that he's looking for a village wife. I trust our son. You can't find good wife from the town." another woman piped in.

"Ah my sister, town women are wicked ones. They will eat their husband's money and still cheat on them. *Tufiakwa!* " she spat on the floor.

Tears stung my eyes as I watched the so called Chief's son get out of the car. It reminded me of Obi. The day he was taking me back to the village, he said that he only wanted to visit Mama. Mama welcomed him but he stashed all my luggages on the floor near Mama's hut and said that he can't marry again. He said that am dirty and he can't bear to stay with me. I cried and begged him but he refused to take me back. He drove off and left our property. A week later, I heard that he married Chika. I cried furiously. Mama tried to find out what happened but I told her that my only regret is that I never told him that I love him.

## ONE SQUARE EACH

Ogige market is not as busy as it was since the lockdown was enforced. Things are getting very expensive and some people are struggling to get by. I am one of those struggling for my family to get by. I stared at the wrapped akamu. They are worth thirty naira but the seller sells it at fifty naira. I bargained but she didn't bat an eyelash. She told me to go if I couldn't afford it. Before the lockdown, I owned a fast-food restaurant. It was doing so well because of the late workers that usually come in for beer, pepper soup and suya. It was also doing well because of the girls I employed. They usually go home with one of the rich men thereby adding bonus to my money.

Nowadays, the government enforced lockdown has curtailed business for me. The girls has gone back to their families and my restaurant is under lock and key, not mine though. I never believed that the so called disease that has been plaguing our country and the entire world is real. Even Ebola didn't crack our country's surface and they expect us, the common people, to believe them. My money in my bank has reduced to five percent of it's worth. My husband was affected the most; he's a bricklayer and bricklayers were the first to be out of business. The small income he brought from work stopped and my money was used to support the family.

Our family, a family of six is still under development. My three daughters are just nine, seven and five years old and my son is still two. They need the food better than me and my husband but my husband doesn't seem to think so. Whenever the meal doesn't go in his favour, he would grumble and shout obscenities at me. He never hits me neither does he hit the children but I can tell from his bloodshot eyes that he wanted to. He wanted to enslave us and eat the meals for himself. He always went to bed hungry as well as me but you don't see me complaining. If not for anything, I should put up a fight because it's my income that is used to fend for this family.

I bought one wrapped akamu and headed towards the Barrow pushers. My daughters have been trying to get money by selling ripe mangoes. We usually get five hundred naira per day but that doesn't seem to satisfy my husband. It seems as if nothing could satisfy my husband nowadays.

Okpa is hard to find nowadays. I can't relate with the sellers on this one because okpa is the daily breakfast for families who can't afford those English breakfast the rich seem to like. Without okpa, the poor families will have nothing to eat. Today, I couldn't find okpa as usual and I don't have money to buy bread. I contemplated what we are to eat as breakfast. We can't eat akamu on its own because it would be tasteless and we won't be satisfied. I thought of eating it together with akara or fried potatoes or fried yam. Either way, we will have something to eat.

Coming back home, I felt the familiar brewing of dissatisfaction in my tummy. It reminded me what I always wanted when I was younger and what I never got. When I was younger, I dreamed of my own home. My rich young husband will own a company based in Lagos and I will own a fast food restaurant. We will be blessed with three kids and we will live in a two storey building. I will decorate the compound with sweet smelling flowers and my children will grow up learning English as their first language.

My version of a husband was a very handsome man, fair in complexion. He will have kind eyes that would make me blush when he looks at me. He would have red lips and his nose would be pointed. He would be tall and he would be so gentle that I will fall on his feet. That was a dream long forgotten.

Instead through out my younger days after I dropped out of secondary school, the fair handsome guys that came for me only wanted hard and fast sex. I wanted that to at the time and I prayed for God's mercy and grace that I will find someone among them. They came and went like water poring out of a coriander. They didn't want me for me. I guess at the time, I was a *congie* (desire to have sex) removal. My mates got married and left the village leaving me with sparse men who looked my way with brown teeth and bloodshot eyes. I swore that I will never marry a man like that. But here I am, saddled with a brown teeth and bloodshot-eyed fellow.

I don't know if he ever loved me. He bought food and clothes for my mother and always helped her in the farm. I knew that he is a bricklayer but I still married him and here we are. After the marriage, we left the village and lived in a two room apartment. The rent was decent and I was able to achieve my dream of establishing a fast food restaurant. He remained a bricklayer and I think he wants to remain a bricklayer for the rest of his life.

As I approached my home, I saw a Jeep leaving our house and my husband staring behind it. I stared at him for a while. Has he also turned into a love sick fool, staring after a Jeep like that, I wondered. The Jeep by passed me and I saw a young girl being restrained from the Jeep's lowered mirror. I ignored the Jeep and walked towards my husband. He turned towards me, leveled me with a gaze that could chill the bones and left through the front door. I shrugged at his strange behaviour and entered the house.

I prepared the akamu and we sat around the plate, taking a piece of akara, eating it and spooning the akamu after it. I noticed that Adaku, my last daughter didn't join us and I asked Amara and Ogechi about it. They said that they haven't seen her. My husband made a sound of disapproval and said,

"She's better of gone anyway. This meal can't feed the six of us."


Nobody said anything afterwards. We were so greedy for the food that we forgot to feed Chetachi, my son and the last born. He couldn't keep up with grown ups and he cried afterwards. I didn't care that he did neither did I care that Adaku hasn't shown up in the afternoon. The other girls went to sell mangoes and I sat on the stool outside watching pedestrians walking up and down the road.


My husband left the house and I went into our room to search it. I don't know what am searching for but I felt like I will know it when I see it. In one of his clothes, I found wads of cash all in one thousand naira note. I knew I couldn't just sit and count it but I know by looking at it, it's more than a hundred thousand.


Where did he get that kind of cash?

I put it back into his shirt pocket, got back to the veranda and sat on the side stool. I didn't want to believe it but I knew what he had done. He has sold Adaku for money. I didn't feel sad for the loss of Adaku. Adaku was like a burden when we were six in number. She would be better off a slave than a part of our family. In the evening, we ate local jellof rice made with red oil. I didn't ask my husband for the money. I didn't tell him that I took three wads of cash from his stash and he didn't notice. I know that he is as greedy as I am when it comes to money and our family continued to live in poverty while stash of money were pilled in my wrapper and in his shirt pocket.

## BAD CRAMPS

"Oluchi, where are you? We are late for church."


I sat on the bathtub clutching my stomach. Earlier in the morning, I felt pain around my stomach but at the time, I felt like I could endure. But as I finished bathing, the pain hit me so hard that I lay crumpled on the bathtub. I knew that I couldn't hold it. The pain made it seem like a bucktooth is eating away my stomach tissue little by little.

"Mum, I need panadol."

"What is it?"

"My stomach...ó narū m aru."


Mum left the bathroom and came back with two tablets of Panadol. I took them and forced myself to stand up.


I can do this.

I tied my scarf tightly and zipped my ankle boots. I pushed through as I went downstairs, using anything to distract me from my stomach. It seems to have calm down but I could still feel the pain. We filed up and got into the car.

St. Peter's Church main building has never failed to marvel me. Whenever I see the building, I find myself considering what it's really made of, bricks, cement? With time, the building has undergone some renovation in certain areas but the original structure still stood. I never asked mum or dad about the structure. I never knew the reason why I didn't. Maybe I wanted to keep marvelling at the beauty of the building or maybe am scared that I would get a simple answer. All in all, I still marvel at the Church's main building. Sometimes, I wonder if it's the work of our colonial masters; if they wanted to leave their mark. If that was their intention, they did a job well done.

Coming out of the car wasn't as organized as when we were getting into the car. Chigozie, the youngest among us jumped off the car and ran all the way to wisdom hall to meet with his friends. Emeka, the eldest child left the car quietly and went towards the Church's main building. Amezie, who is two years older than me bumped my left shoulder while he ran all the way to the main building. I'm twelve years old and I don't need to attend the children's mass going on in wisdom hall. So, I trudged my way up the stairs and into the Church.

I sat in the third row bench over looking the window. Looking at the Church building outside, it gives the impression of a one storey building but it's a typical bungalow. The Church has a high ceiling and low hanging bulbs and fans. It is divided into three segment: the middle one houses the high ceiling while the other two has the low ceilings. I hate staying at the lower ceiling segments but I had no choice today, we came after the gospel has been read.

Sitting on the pew, I felt my stomach cramp up again. It hit me like a blow and I clutched it. I couldn't stand up during the points when we should have been standing during mass. No one gave me the look but then, no one noticed me. At the end of mass, I stood up, glad that I would be going home. Someone tapped me lightly on my shoulder and I looked back. It's a dark, tall guy and he has a scrowl on his face. He pointed at my skirt and I mouthed, what. He leans towards me and said,

"There is blood on your skirt."

"Oh, okay."

I looked at the back of my skirt. Red stains were spread around one area. My pants felt heavy and the junction were my two legs met felt gummy but that was none of my concern. My stomach cramps has started again. It seemed as if an alien has started building a mini Church using my stomach tissues.

"I will tie it with my scarf later. Thank you, sir."

The man stared at me in disbelief but I didn't concern myself with him anymore. Someone else tapped me in my left shoulder and I looked up. This person is a lady and she sat down quietly, gesturing for me to sit as well. I didn't want to sit because I felt uncomfortable. But I ignored my comfort and sat down.

"Do you know what is happening to you?"

"There is nothing happening to me, ma."

She leans down and gestured for me to come nearer. I raised an eyebrow and shifted towards her.

"Is this your first menstrual period?"

At first, I couldn't grasp what she was saying but when I did, I felt like melting on the floor. In my state of mortification, I turned towards the guy who is currently making his way towards the door. Then, I covered my face in embarrassment.

"I'm so sorry...," I mumbled, "... This is my first time. All I felt was the pain in my stomach. I didn't know."

"Did you come with your parents?"

"Yes, ma"

"Call their numbers. Let me let them know of your condition."

I told her and she called mum. Mum rushed into the Church and ran towards me. She hugged me and I felt like bawling.

"I'm so sorry…, " mum stuttered, addressing the woman, "… I'm not always like this. This is my daughter's first time."

"It is okay. I am a teacher at university secondary school. I understand your situation," the woman smiled kindly.

"Thank you for helping her."

"You are welcome."

The lady left the Church and mum told me that dad went to buy pads. I waited with mum. I laid my head on her shoulder and stared at the altar. When I first heard about period, I was so excited for my own to start. I thought about how mine would start, dreaming about how I would react in various occasion if it ever started at that place. I never imagined that my first period would be in Church without a pad to protect me. This is the most humiliating moment in my entire life.

Dad came running into the Church, followed on his heels by Emeka. He didn't come into the Church but I saw him staring at me. I went to the back of the pew and put the pad on, cringing at the amount of blood on my pants and how it smelled unpleasant. I tied my scarf around my hip and we trudged our way to the car. Our car is the only one in the compound but I didn't care. Before we got into the car, Emeka stopped me and said,

"Whenever you need help calculating your cycle, call me. I'm an expert."

**WHAT IS WRONG, IS WRONG**

Hunger was what I was used to. The title was like a dirt smeared on my cheek. I hated that word and the emotions that came with it. It wasn't easy but this world wasn't easy to begin with. Life was too difficult. A fresh graduate of electrical engineering just five years ago, I was the pride of my family. It was very emotional to be honest. We weren't rich but I made it. I did it but the problem resides in getting a well-paying job.

While I was in the university, I went through simple jobs here and there knowing that I would make it in life. I would hear fellowship students preach about how we will make it in life if we just read, be good christian, dress well, avoid immorality and all what not and I laughed. Christianity seems like a sort of weak spot for anyone to me. Don't get me wrong.

I go to church, listen to the world of God, scream and shout whenever it's prayer time, touch people or maybe fall on the floor if need be and speak in tongues but that's just for show. Sometimes, the church helps people like us without any money and so, I've got to work with one Christian faith.

My problem began after school. The path I had thought would be my path to freedom; to building rich relations with rich people and politicians like I had told my friends back at school. It didn't happen immediately but after, I managed to get a palm-wine tapping job because I found someone willing to teach me.

At first, I enjoyed the work; though I never felt fulfilled that it is worth something. I married the woman I was wooing and she gave birth to our first child, a boy. Well, we were as happy as happy can get, living in a bungalow that I built on my own in a large compound.

It wouldn't have really mattered if I hadn't seen Matt, my university school mate. He was riding a jeep when I saw him and he had heard about my palm-wine. It was supposedly sweet and he decided to try it out. He was surprised to see me as the owner. We spoke together and he joked about me being too proud and making a show of knowing everything which I did anyway. He joked about how I made a first class and though he did well, I was a palm-wine tapper while he was a businessman and he ended with, what a small world we live in.

I gave a half chuckle and echoed him. We laughed at how miserable or pitiable I seemed in his eyes and I charged him with a bigger amount than usual and he paid without batting an eyelash. Maybe, his way of letting me know that he could pay for it. I didn't show it but I was bitter.

Ever since then, I did a lot of things, invested in a lot of businesses, even if some seemed like a hoax. I did anything that seemed good and would get a lot of money but many flopped while others gave me very little money.

My wife got very sick leading to a very low drop in the money we had remaining. I couldn't afford the medical care involved and so, we watched her wither away and die. My son caught the sickness too but he seemed to be able to manage it better than my wife. A week later, we buried her with the amount remaining in the bank and I went broke.

Two weeks of scraping by, I had no choice. The choice I made took me many days to follow up with it. I have to admit, I don't really regret it. It was a simple thought. I remember my days back at school. There was this famous verse in the bible that was popular for some reason and it said, we are nothing but empty vessels in the hands of God. I thought that verse was so backward at the time but every time someone quotes that verse, the crowd in the church would go crazy.

Using that, I considered my options. We were starving, no one wants to feed us and my son's getting sicker. I can't keep carrying him everywhere. I've got to live my life as well and so, I made my decision. That must have been the best decision I've ever made. Ever since then, I've been a professional.

I left my town and village. It was a waste of talent if you get my drift. At first, I lived without a reason or purpose. It felt like I really have lost the last humanity I had in me but someone recruited me when he saw my potential. My nickname became Ode. It doesn't really mean anything. It just became my name. My master is Da-Da, short for "down there". A rumor has it that he kills all his girlfriends after one night because he's afraid that they would gossip about his tiny penis.

I know exactly what he does with his girlfriends but on my part, it doesn't really matter. He is rich of course. He has a whole street under his belt and of course, just like the Mexicans call it, he's a drug dealer. But that's why he became my master. He's the only one that knows my secret as I'm his right hand man. For a while now, everything was perfect until we had a run in with the police after he tried to run for governor. Politics is very backward but if it's a sure way to hold power, it doesn't matter. I didn't support him on this but I never told him and we thought that it would be as smooth sailing as every other job we've done.

It happened that his opponent had a strong supporter who happens to be my very good friend and classmate. Seeing this, I could fathom how rich he could be if he were supporting a governor-to-be. I decided to pay him a visit in my Jeep. But of course, I let my boss know that I wanted to recruit him on our side and he gave me the green light. I was happy.

I went there and we exchanged pleasantries. I, with smugness and he, with wide eyes. I wished he would stutter. It would have been miraculous but he didn't. He upheld his part as a gentleman with his beautiful wife and two beautiful grownup daughters. I was jealous of what he had. He had it all and I feel like am still struggling to get something.


Initially, I was there for revenge, maybe kill him and kidnap his family or maybe burn the whole house to the ground but I decided to respect my boss and ask him nicely to join us. He refused out rightly and told me to leave his house. I smiled at him and told him my signature words,

"The apple does not fall far from the tree. You realize that."


It's just my way of telling him to be careful. He was confused but he didn't let it bother him like every of my victims and that night, he and his family met their water loo. I don't need to wish for what he has when he's not around to have more. But I didn't finish in time. I heard sirens from afar and remember thinking, why would the police come to his home by this time. I jumped the fence just in time to see the gate man opening the gates for them and I just knew. He was gone the next day. And like usual, we would have gone about our day but the police just had to arrest me.


They tortured me for a while, asking for answers to questions they asked. I laughed at them. I thought that I would be released soon but that was far-fetched. They were able to retrieve videos from that cursed man's house. It showed exactly what I did to them and I watched it as the police officers lamented on how changed and decayed the world has become. It reminded me of what I did to my son.


We were starving and I had no choice. I took him to the bush behind our house and built a fire. I placed him on the fire and watched him cook. His flesh burnt and gave off this charcoal burning smell. I cut his limbs little by little and roasted them. It was meat and I was greedy even though I was the only one eating it. The fleshy limbs tasted like cow meat and I wanted to eat more. I didn't eat the skull. I believed that the skull had memories and they might affect my memory.


I left my village after that and lived like a scavenger. I would try to eat bread but it was never tasty. I wanted human meat and so, I killed mad people before I started killing anybody that would be walking on the road at night. That was how I met Da-Da. He watched me kill someone and told me that he would deliver human meat to me if I worked for him. And I did. I ate all his girlfriends and I got rich too.


For my good ol'annoying classmate, I was boiling his daughter when I heard the sirens. I had planned to cook them in their house. I used a machete to behead each of them. My good ol'friend while he was watching TV, his wife while she was cooking along with their eldest daughter and their youngest daughter while she was in bed maybe sleeping or listening to music because she had her ear pods in her ear.

I haven't started cooking yet. I just threw in his first daughter's meat and I heard the sirens. I ate the gate-man for breakfast the next day but I couldn't finish it at dinner because the police arrested me that night. After watching the video, I laughed and said,

"Does it really matter? Humans are meat in the eyes of God. Only those with the power to kill can harvest this raw meat."

And so it began, the judge sentenced me to death by firing squad. Da-Da didn't glance at me like I thought he would and that triggered it. I screamed at him and told him that he would go down with me. I wrote down everything he did as well as his acquaintances and every man under him. Before they shot me, I remembered my son's meat. No matter what they say, his meat was the best but then, I thought, I would never know how my wife tastes like before I heard a gunshot.

**LOVE CAN BE BLIND**

I've always known that I was pretty. Pretty enough to attract an *already-made* man. I had the hips, round hips that I would prefer stayed in tight jeans, trousers, shorts and skirts. My bottom is as large as my hips. They were not my greatest assets but they could attract any man if I swing them to the tune of any music. My thin tiny stomach could be my greatest asset. I've always loved to rock it in crop tops or just stay naked in my underwear in my room staring at it and imagining what my future husband would think of it when he sees it.

My breasts are my favorite asset. It's large, voluminous and round. Sometimes, I can't handle it and I would wish that I had a smaller breast to look after but after seeing how hungry men stared at it on the streets or in classes, I would flaunt it and be so proud of myself.

My figure is something someone would call a figure eight. I have every physique a girl could ask for but there's just one boy that hasn't given me a look. He's very handsome and very wealthy, in my opinion. He's not a student but he comes to my class sometimes to talk to his older brother. I've tried everything I could to get his attention. It's like his attention is always fixated on that stupid elder brother of his. So, I hated his elder brother.

I didn't want to talk to him or maybe try to get him speak to his younger brother for me. It would really hurt my pride if I did it because I have so many admirers in my class excluding that elder brother of his. The two were the same but the elder brother is not handsome at all.

He has big black lips that are noticably, red in between. His haircut is always *amala*, a haircut that involves barbing off every atom of hair. He's always in need of help and not as cool as his younger brother. He's too tall and lanky and he's dark in complexion. He carries a messenger bag everywhere that he wears across his shoulder and he rarely wears any new clothing.

His younger brother is fair and tall but not that tall. He's not lanky and he dresses like a teenage boy, always on sneakers, jeans or joggers, and t-shirts. He usually styles his hair and not just amala. He has dark eyes and usually has his lips in wed-lips.

The elder brother is an *over-do* christian. His phone has every single bible passage on it and before any lecture, he would suggest that everyone should pray. It usually gets on my nerves. He's not really that intelligent. He answers some questions thrown at him but he fails some of them and he answers like someone who is not fluent in English.

But he speaks Igbo language, one of the languages in Nigeria, like an indigene of Nsukka, a town in Enugu, Nigeria. I call it *concentrated Igbo* because he speaks like an ancient mother. I've never heard his younger brother speak before but I know with his assets, his voice would be smooth, kind and maybe somewhat rough and husky but low and more feminine than his elder brother.

Today, I have decided that I wouldn't stay back and wait for him to notice me. Since the day I met him, I have only sat closer to his elder brother but not so close as to seem desperate. I would wear a plunging neckline, attracting every male species including the lecturers but neither him nor his elder brother would notice me. And just like that, I would be invisible in a class of hungry males.

In my culture, clothes like tiny shorts and crop tops or mini skirts are somewhat forbidden. It's not written in any law but it's like an unwritten agreement between elderly women that are passed down to the younger generation. Even knowing this didn't stop me from wearing them to class. A few lecturers that do not tolerate "indecent clothing" would walk me out of the class before classes began or during classes. And still, I'm yet to receive my due. I refuse to sit and wait till he notices me.

I didn't dress indecently this time. I have my assets; I just had to highlight every minute detail, make them more noticeable. Sometimes he catches me unawares by coming on a date I didn't take note of but he has a routine. I don't know why he took it upon himself to visit his older brother on intervals but his routine is a big advantage for me. I've been stalking them for a while and even if his pit-stops are usually in the classroom, he also visits him in his hostels. I can't go there. It would make my stalking suspicious.

That day in class, I put lip gloss on my lips and adjusted my top to fit my breasts. I sat close to his brother in a sluttery pose, chewing my gum and making sure it doesn't stick to the roof of my mouth. His brother glanced at me for a while. I'm sure he's wondering why I'm sitting the way I am or maybe why am trying to catch his attention. I rolled my eyes and thought, what a pity. If he were half as handsome as his brother, maybe I would consider him but I would rather live with mice than date him.

His brother walked into the room as usual and I sat up. He glanced at me for a minute but then, he turned back to his ugly brother. I was beyond livid. Are you that oblivious, I thought but then, a thought occurred to me. Isn't he a cutie to have pretended not to notice me but is inwardly giving me the green light?

I glanced at his brother and found him looking at me with a frown. I shot him a look and looked away. What's his problem, I thought. But then another thought occurred to me. What if he's trying to avoid his brother while giving me a sign that we could meet after he leaves. I smiled.

I stole a look at him and found him looking at me. I smiled and winked at him while biting my lips. He stared at me for a while. The wrinkling of his forehead and furrowing of his eyebrows showed that he's frowning or concentrating on something. But then, he looked down at my plunging neckline, down to my voluminous boobs. I smiled and adjusted it to his liking. His eyebrows shot to the roof and I smiled again.

I stood up and walked out of the classroom. I stood in a dark corner and waited, knowing fully well that he would pass that way. When he was about to pass me, I shot out my hand, held his arm and dragged him into the small room. I pushed him towards the wall and said,

"You are playing hard to get on purpose. I will show you what you are missing."

I held him down thinking that he would cooperate but he decided to fight till the end. He gave out a lady-like scream and I laughed. What's with this guy? He doesn't act like a guy at all. I tried to grab his penis but there was nothing to grab. He was struggling and shouting that I should leave him alone and I was struggling trying to tame him.

I figured pulling the zip of his trousers or maybe the trousers itself would compel him to obedience. I checked with my fingertips and his trouser clearly has no zips. I shrugged, inwardly and thought, I would have to pull his trousers off. But as I did so, the doors opened to my classmates staring at me. It made me pause which gave him ample opportunity to throw me off him.

"What is wrong with you?" he screamed in a lady-like voice.

"Oh shut up. You like it but you pretend like you don't." I said, trying to fix myself and pretend like I'm not embarrassed by what he did.

"Are you a lesbian or what...and here I thought you were trying to seduce my fiance." he said.

Hold up, I thought. What did he mean by that statement?

"Excuse me, are you a girl?" I asked.

"Yes. Who did you think I was? He's my fiance." she said.

My eyes bulged out of my eye sockets. For a while, the visits, the raised eyebrows, her inability to look at me as a woman started to make sense. She's a tomboy, I thought. Was I delusional? Do I want a nice, homey guy so bad that I imagined that she was one? It could be that. Her behavior was deceiving. But I can't accuse someone for something I had mistaken all on my own.

For a while, everywhere was quiet. Then, they started laughing. I was so embarrassed that I didn't know what to do with myself. Her fiance was laughing as well and she joined in the laughter. I've been pranked. I released a breath and with my last dignity, I left the restroom.

Ever since then, my classmates would always poke fun at me. I dressed more modestly and paid more attention to people and my classes. Whenever she visits her fiance, she would speak to me. She rarely visits as often as she did in the past and that is because she felt intimidated by me from the very beginning. She had thought that I wanted to steal her man and so, she made frequent visits to his classes to keep an eye on me herself.

Sometimes, I would wonder what made me fantasize about her in the past. Was she handsome or did she have a feature that I would want in a man? Or maybe, she seemed so far away and I couldn't get her no matter how hard I tried. Or maybe, she just looked like a boy, a different boy from every other person I have ever encountered.

## WHAT SHOULD BE CALLED CRAZY

I was born quiet like those butterflies floating in the wind, like the early morning dew creeping without a sound, like those soundless moths flying towards bright lights. I was born in a hospital like every other child and like every other child, I was expected to learn.

Know my surroundings, my environment and master them like any other child. I was supposed to be normal, growing from an infant to a clueless child. From a clueless child to a playful child. From a playful child to a mindless teenager. From a mindless teenager to a tactful teenager. From a tactful teenager to a growing adult. From a growing adult to a mature adult.

That was my responsibility. That was what nature had given me, has given every babes all and sundry. But why was I different? As abnormal as a butterfly that can't float in the wind, as stupid as a dew that drums the rooftops to announce it's presence or as noisy as the moth that flies towards any bright light.

When I was born, mama said that I had the creepiest honey coloured eyes, something that my great-great-great-great, I don't know how great, grandfather had. It had been lost and they believed that my multiple great-grandfather had reincarnated himself in me. Maybe he just wanted to live a modern life because he never had the chance when he was alive. Or maybe he wanted to creep everyone out because they were horrible to him when he was alive.

Whichever case, mama thought that it was a blessing to see multiple great grand-father again. Or that was the case until they knew that they had asked the unasked. At first, while growing up, I wasn't able to crawl. They would bend my kneecap and expect me to crawl on the floor but I will lie there, drawing invisible images on thin air.

They decided that I wasn't meant to crawl. Mama was in fact excited that I wasn't able to crawl. She said that I would be a special child like those children that would skip a growth stage and be something special in the future like a doctor, a lawyer or an engineer. Anything that would require studying books. I was little back then and I didn't know the high hopes she had placed on me. Maybe if I had known, I would have tried harder, fought it until it became mine to keep.

After I turned two, Mama's high hopes for me shattered. I couldn't walk and I couldn't crawl either. Was I lame? The doctor said no and that in due time, I will learn how to walk. Mama hated it. I would hear her cry every night and papa would console her. They would blame it on their enemies and they would reassure themselves that I am only a special child. Special children shouldn't grow fast. They grow very slowly to fool their future enemies into thinking that they are less better than them.

Walking wasn't the only problem back then. Before I turned one, I learned how to write faster than I learned how to speak. Writing came easy to me but the problem is that I write with my left hand. Mama called it an abomination. Aka-ekpe, the left hand, is not meant to be noticed or seen. It can only be used when something happens to the right hand.

She forced me to learn how to write with my right hand but I couldn't even hold a pen or a spoon with my right hand. It was practically useless, like a limp noodle. My left hand helped me a lot but mama cried. She would lament and talk like she's speaking to someone in person,

"Why do I have a son like this? Take him away. I don't need him."

I could understand her but I couldn't say a word. Unlike every other babes, I haven't spoken my first word to my parents. It's not that I withheld saying something. Maybe it's how sad mama and papa seem whenever they look at me. It forbade me to say anything. I was two years old when I spoke my first words and they were, "Don't cry, mama." She wasn't as pleased as I thought she would be. She was angry and mad at me. She screamed at me and I shrank within myself. I never wanted to talk again.

Talking made mama angry but it made papa happy. I only spoke when papa is around because he won't yell at me like mama or stare at me like every other person. I took my first steps when I was five. I was happy and I looked at mama to see her reaction. She was neither happy nor sad. She shook her head and left the room. Papa clapped for me and I clapped too. I wanted to walk only for papa but it wasn't possible.

Mama sent me on any errand she could and she made me talk by flogging me whenever I don't. I don't hate mama but she was making it hard. I don't like her at all but I wanted her to be proud. My siblings alienated me by playing amongst themselves. I don't know why. I have tried all sorts of things to try and make them play with me but they would run away whenever they saw me coming. Very soon, papa stopped being nice. He would usually exclaim,

"Chinedu, stop acting like a child. You are fifteen for God's sake."

I didn't act like a child. He just can't see it. My siblings grew up like a normal child would and mama was proud of them. But I didn't get her approval. I never did. The future couldn't have been anymore bright. I was eighteen when mama sent me to the borehole to fetch water with one bucket. She has never done that. Usually, she would give me two buckets, a 50 liter gallon or a big bowel. But this time, she gave me a small bucket that had no handle and has broken by the sides. I didn't complain. I remember that anytime I go to fetch water, my back or my neck would hurt. I thought she acknowledged that and decided to give me an insignificant bucket. I was so wrong.

I got back from the borehole, sweaty and water from the bucket spilling on my hair and clothes. The house was lively and I thought that we had something to celebrate. Thinking about the fried chicken, jollof or fried rice and creamy salad made me salivate. I walked faster but the bucket on my head slipped and fell. It broke in half and I cried. Mama wouldn't be pleased. She would scream at me and make me carry those heavy burdens to the borehole as well as doubling my house chores. I took the broken pieces and walked up to the house. I knocked at the gate and no one replied. I knocked and knocked but no one said anything. I sat down in front of the gate and waited.

I waited until dawn. I couldn't sleep. Chiekube was the first person that came out of the gate and he spotted me but he didn't say anything. I was excited to see him. He was my first breath of sunshine in a heavy storm and I ran towards him.

"Chiekube, I've been waiting since last night. Where are mama and papa? I am sorry I broke the bucket but I can get another water for mama if she would give me another bucket."

Chiekube pushed me aside like he was trying to swat an annoying fly and he left me. I didn't know what to do. Should I follow him or should I wait? My fingers were scratching my head. I didn't have lice or dandruff but that was a habit I picked up. The more I scratched, the more confused I became until I was pacing the gate. I was biting my fingernails while my left hand scratched my head.

People stared at me and some of them stopped and pointed. What were they looking at? Do I look like a scavenger? I screamed at them. I screamed till my voice was hoarse. Whenever anyone pointed, I screamed and chased that person but it didn't matter what happened. Neither mama nor papa came out to speak with me.

Chiekube stared wide-eyed at me before running into the house and locking the gate. I stayed in front of the house for three days without food and water but nobody came out of the house. They only did when they needed something or papa had to go to work. After these torturous days, I knew that they didn't want me in their lives. They wanted me to go.

I couldn't go to school because I can't relate to my classmates and I can't talk to my teachers. I don't write or read in school and my teachers are always frustrated with me. I can't play with my peers in my neighborhood and I can't play with my siblings. All I can do is work but apparently, that wasn't enough for mama.

I cried and cried as I left my village. No one glanced at me or asked me why I was crying. They wanted me to go as well. It doesn't matter. I never liked them. I want them gone as well. I want them dead especially mama and my siblings. Papa would be flogged and thrown in prison. He would stay there without any light like those men that would be locked up in those Philippine movies on AIT channel. And he will rot there.

I glared at the ground that was moving because I was walking. I wanted to sound like those women in the Philippine movies but I doubt I could ever sound like them. I'm useless and probably stupid like mama would say about me.

I walked and walked. I don't know where I was but I have not eaten anything since the last time I ate which was before I was sent to fetch water. I couldn't eat even if I tried. My lips were dry and my nose ached. It felt dry and stuffy. My eyes were dry and my skin irritates me. It was a far cry from what I tolerated at my house but I would prefer this to my former house.

It's very constant now. I don't know how many days, weeks, months or years but they seem oddly familiar to me. All I knew was how people grew, those that were familiar to me as kids, I watched as they grew up into adults. At first, someone would stop and give me a note, clothes or a flask of food. It's like they just wanted to help or they just noticed someone different from them and thought that he needed something to complete him. I appreciated it at first but then, the whispers started.

"He's from Enugu-ezike."

"I heard that he was cursed by a *dibia*, native doctor."

"I heard that his evil relatives tossed him out of his home."

"I heard that he used his girlfriend in a money making ritual and was never the same."

"I heard that he was part of a cult that believed in sacrificing old women to their god."

"I heard that he's a *yahoo boy*, money making by dubious means, and his time of enjoyment is gone. Now, he's undergoing a time of suffering."

"I heard he killed his best friend and used him for money making ritual but his best friend cursed him and he was never the same."

Those whispers caused confusion within me. I don't know where they came from. The more I bit my fingernails, scratched my head and paced, the more confused I got and eventually, I screamed. I chased after anyone that looked at me. They are criminals, alien creatures that don't deserve to live on earth. I threw their darn flask back at them, their clothes mean nothing to me. I will live this earth scavenging. I screamed at them and threw stones at them.

Ever since then, they avoided me. They would never stare at me. They refuse to speak to me and they refuse to initiate close contact with me. Dubious, I thought. They were dubious people.

I never grew taller nor did I shrink. I remained the same like the unchanging time. No matter how many man-made clocks, seasons and celebrations pass, time will never change. I am that time. My clothes never changed and I think I grew out my hair. I scratch my head often but not as much as when people stare at me. My fingernails were crooked and they sometimes have caked brown sands from digging up termites, ants or millipedes to eat or just digging for the fun of it.

I am laughing now. I laugh at anything that gives me joy. The little boy that threw his pen into the pond. The man that kicked his tire because his car stopped working. The woman that struggled with her *gele*, hair tie and heels as she ran to church. The little kids that ran after cars, screaming at them all the time. Those little things were so funny that I couldn't help but laugh.

My legs were long. I never noticed that. I sat close to one of the pillars and watched as people trooped through the gates. They were different in a way. Like the smallest person that would rather lie in someone's arms then walk to the biggest person that would match towards the gates like there's an award if they crossed the gates successfully.

One, two, three, four, I counted aloud but someone blocked me; a young girl. She gave me one of those paper things people hold nowadays. I have never seen her before. She tied her hair in two pigtails and had only two teeth when she smiles. Then, with a squeaky voice, she said,

"Daddy said that I should give you that."

Daddy? I thought. I have heard that word before. I know I have but I don't remember when. I gave a croak-like laughter that ended in a dry cough. The little girl shifted and glanced behind her. I wanted her to see what would happen after the cough. I wanted her to be around while I coughed. But she moved backwards. I didn't know that I had gotten up until she turned around and started running.

I started chasing her while trying to hold my cough until the last minute. She has to see it, I thought. My cough means something to me. It has to mean something to her too. But the cough ended and I spit out the blood. I stopped running and whipped my palms on my shorts. I felt like crying. Why wouldn't she just look at me? She was screaming as she ran and someone held her, an elderly woman. She turned towards me and I froze. I know her. I turned away and left the compound.

Red, blue, green, yellow, they went in a blur. I fell on the floor and stared at the blue sky. I know that it's blue but it just seemed ash like. It was that colour whenever it would rain droplets of water. I felt a drop of water like that salty liquid from my eyes. One, two, three and it started falling like a storm. I couldn't get up. I laid there remembering her face. Mama, she looked older now but her eyes were the same thing. I'm not happy like usual but am not sad. It feels tranquil, like the early morning breeze during the rainy season.

I was at peace and I felt better than I had. Maybe I just had to see mama before I would be at peace or maybe, I just had to see how well or how sad she was doing before I would be at peace. When I looked at her eyes, they were not happy but they were not sad either. She had this reservation within her like she doesn't regret it but she doesn't have to regret it to like it. Or maybe, this is just wistful thinking.

## LIFE'S MISTAKE

The rain pelted along with the steady drumbeats of the music Ada is listening to on the radio. She glanced towards her parents in tow. Her dad was whistling and drumming his fingers on the steering wheel as he maneuvered through the traffic. Her mum sat quietly, maybe listening to the music on the radio like Ada. They seem like a normal family going back home from work and school.


The rain fell harshly on the roof of the car unaware of Ada's fear of road accidents. She held onto a shred of hope that her dad is not a novice in driving a car under a heavy rain. Her mum is with her as well, she reasoned. Her dad will never try to harm her mum intentionally.


There was a traffic hold up and for a while, the car has not moved from its position. Ada sighed in relief. She didn't care what the hold up was about so long as her father toned down his speed. She stared at her side window. The window, in question was glazed over by the dense vapour due to the heavy rain. She wiped it but couldn't see clearly because the dense vapour was settled on both sides of the window.


Someone flagged down her father's car. Rain water dripped from the man's dark face making Ada think about the boys in the boys quarter back home. Whenever they came out from the bathroom, they had water dripping down their bare chest and a towel tied around their middle to cover their manhood. But still, Ada saw the pressure from their pubic area push towards the towel, straining whenever they see her watching them.

She never pulled her eyes away whenever they made eye contact. She liked watching them half naked. They put the Korean boys to shame because whilst the boys had hardened chest, beards and abs to show, the Korean boys had slim almost thin bodies, no beards and flat stomachs. But they had the beauty of gods that overshadowed their physical features whilst the boys were sun burnt and ugly looking.

The man shoved his head into the car as if to prevent rain from beating his head, instead he wet the car seat with the rain water dripping from his face.

"You have to turn back now." he said

"Why?" her father asked.

"There have been an accident. A terrible accident." the man said, as if that would make her father tear a race away from the accident.

"What happened?" her father asked

The man spoke long drawn out Igbo but she had understood bits and pieces of what he said.

The accident was between a tanker and a bus. The tanker had been backing out and the bus refused to wait for it. The bus driver might have seen an opening, the man said and he took it with a dash of speed but the driver of the tanker backed out too quickly and they collided. No one survived in the bus but the tanker driver is alive and well.

The man spat on the tarred floor outside her father's window as if to clear excess hatred for the bus driver. He endangered the lives of so many promising people. He probably is in hell suffering for it while the ghost of the people will continue to wonder about the scene of the accident.

Ada didn't think the bus driver would immediately go to hell. She's sure the man talking about it has not lost a relative. If he had, he would be crying, she reasoned and he wouldn't be here guiding the traffic and talking nonsense about what is not his business. A part of her wanted to see the scene of the accident but she knew what would happen if she does. She would feel nauseated and wouldn't speak another word about an accident, even a spill of water on their tiled floor.

Her mother's voice was quiet when she asked,

"Do you know another road to Ikenga?"

The man nodded, vigorously spilling rain water on her father's tailored trousers and the steering wheel.

"Go through Enugu road and make a right turn at the first intersection. Do you know Orban girl's road?"

Her father nodded vigorously as well as if to affirm that he knew the road all too well.

"I do." he said.

Ada knew that he knew the road. She has gone to that school, her alma mater. She didn't like it all that much but her friends made her stay bearable.

"Good..." the man said, "...that road leads to a T-junction. If you make a left turn, you are at Ikenga."

"Thank you." her mother said

While her father reversed, she kept a wary eye on her window trying to see pass the dense fog. Maybe she could glimpse the accident before her dad backed out.

She did see the scene of the accident and her father couldn't back out quickly because numerous cars tried to reverse at the same time blocking the traffic. She stared at the mangled, bloodied bodies. A man laid on the road with torn blue jeans soaked in blood. He had only one hand, the other probably detached from him during the accident and his face was bashed in.

That man was probably right, the bus driver has endangered many people. He might have thought only of himself while trying to bypass the tanker or maybe there were other reasons like he had a pregnant wife to get to. She can't be sure of it. She has been on a bus before and she knows how reckless a bus driver can be.

In one of the cars, a small face was pressed onto the car window. She seemed excited by the accident whilst Ada felt like retching. She had ate akara and fried yam and washed it with a drink of orange juice. She wondered what would come out if she vomited in the car. Will her dad scold her or would he take her twenty three year old self as been immature? But she didn't vomit. Instead, she wondered what the little girl's view on the accident that made her so excited. Maybe it's just childlike innocence. What would she do when she grows up and remember this accident? Would she be apologetic or would she turn up her nose and say,

"That happened years ago, why should I be bothered by it now."

She thought about it as her father drove them home. She thought about the smashed bus and the tanker that might only have a dent from the accident. The bus driver did put the lives of the people in the bus in danger. But he also died from the impact. She guessed, in somepeople's perspective, the bus driver deserved death. But no one would know if a boko Haram subordinate was in the bus, a thief or a kidnapper. If they had known, would they have congratulated the bus driver or would they still condemn him?

## GREED?

She saw him today. She knew she had a debt to pay but she hadn't estimated this much. She never liked the pleasure. He did though. He released all his pent up emotions within him on her. She was his release and him, her nightmare. She had always only wanted one thing, a loving family. A man who would love her and four children, two boys and two girls.

Is that too much to ask?


Growing up in a farm settlement wasn't easy. She didn't have all the necessities of life but at least, she had shelter and a decent meal everyday. Her house was only but a thatched hut where she lived with her father and her two elder brothers. Her mother left them after giving birth to her and she had to take over cooking at an early stage.


Life was hard but she went to school. It would have been an achievement for her but she just had to make one costly mistake that lead to her being a secondary school dropout. If only she had known that her father would die, she wouldn't have done it.


He stood in front of her house in all his glory smoking a cigarette and staring at God knows what, maybe wondering why he has to keep up with the young lady currently making her way towards him. She was coming back from her evening jog when she saw him. She does nothing nowadays. Money comes and goes like rain does in a rainy season and she would never know where it came from. She knew he was into illegal business, maybe drugs but she couldn't question him on it. He wasn't married and so, she doesn't have to deal with an annoying housewife but she doesn't like her position either.

She stopped and stared at him. He seemed tired by the way he leant on the wall of her house. He had gifted this house to her after lying to her and forcing her to leave all she's ever known. She's twenty-five and yet, it doesn't seem like she's paid the debt in full.

"Where were you?" he asked as he threw the cigarette on the floor, with a flick of his finger and stamps on it.

"I was going on my evening jog." she replied.

"You know that I don't want you to work." he said, stroking her cheek.

"I know." she replied, pretending to purr as he stroked her cheek.


She could play the role of a dutiful housewife or a girlfriend if he wants her to. She has grown use to him and she's afraid that she's attached to him to the point that she can't live without him; but that won't change the fact that she finds him disgusting. He doesn't allow her to do anything. She has started taking online classes under a different name because she thought that she could plan her future without his knowledge on the matter.


He kissed her full on the lips. He smelt of beer, cigar and soap. She let him kiss her. She has never denied him of sex, no matter how nauseating it was. He took her by her hand and tugged her into her house. He laid her on the bed and she removed his clothes. She did it slowly, like he taught her. He had taught her the act of seduction which she's really poor at. But removing his clothes made her seem like she's perfected it. He never complained and she was never worried.

He kissed her again and she succumb to him. She was use to it already and she knew where to touch and what to do. When he entered inside her, she knew the right sound to make so it would seem like she's having a good time. He always seems to be enjoying it; that was only what mattered, apparently.

He shook and shuddered before falling on top of her. She have never experienced the pleasure she read in books or watched on YouTube videos. She never asked why he had a short stamina and why he couldn't hold out for her to have that desired pleasure. She never tried it herself as well. She was too ashamed and embarrassed to try it. It seemed like something another person would do, could do and not something she could or would do.

He laid back on the bed and blinked at her. While smiling, he kissed her neck and said,

"Oluchi, you are my world."

"You are my all as well." she replied to his miniscule praise.

He always says that after each round and it left her wondering why he bothered to speak to her.

"What will I do without you?" he asked.

"I don't know." she replied, honestly.


She has always wondered how her life would have turned out if she didn't listen to him. If she hadn't come for his help and her father had died, would she be a medical doctor? Would she be married? She would never know. He had threatened to kill her elder brothers who were completely oblivious to what was happening and she had to comply. She could still remember the mischievous man that hit on her when she was only sixteen and in SS1.


He had asked her to be his girlfriend countless times but she had refused. When she found out that her father had cancer, she and her brothers started rounding up money for his treatment. He had offered his services and she had declined, knowing his kind. But when her father had coughed out blood during one of his heavy coughs, she had accepted his help.


He paid for her father's treatment but he died a week after being administrated into the hospital. He paid for the funeral and her brothers thanked him. They thought he was a suitor. When she entered senior three, he told her that he had a better school in mind for her and she had gotten so excited. She dropped out of school without a direct entry into any school and he bought an apartment for her. She has been living there ever since and he only comes to have sex with her.


She had thought of stabbing him while he was asleep but her thoughts had wondered to his money. If he were killed, how would she manage herself? She never tried to contact her brothers for fear that he would cut off her pocket money. She obeys him because of the same thing. The money had helped her write her GCE exams, JAMB and screening exams. She's counting on the money to help her through her online classes and personal up keep. Killing him is not an option.


She cuddled him like he wanted and he went to sleep, his head in between her breast, snoring away. This made her imagine her future, what will happen to her if she were to be thrown into the cruel, cold world?


In the background, the girl that waved was played on repeat over and over...

In the busy city,

Bursting with lights and activities,

A girl waved,

She waved at her lost life,

She waved at her sadness,

She waved at her greed,

Her nonchalant attitude and her sorrows,

She waved and waved,

Through every bursting activity,

They all seemed unaware,

That little girl,

That little lost girl,

Waved undeterred,

She smiled,

Her smile entails the heart,

She cried,

Her tears could harden a heart,

She waved at everything,

Everything she could lay her eyes on,

She waved at the motorist as well,

Those that tore through the city roads,

She waved until her sorrows glided to sadness,

Her sadness became grief,

Her grief became pain,

Her pain became a burden,

Her burden became a load,

Her load laid the road to sacrifice,

Her sacrifice laid the road to insanity,

Her insanity laid the road to greed,

Why wouldn't it,

After all she had waved at,

But still a piece of her,

Waved at the closing world,

And to all she could be heard saying,

I'm sorry.

## A LETTER TO MY SPINSTER

Dear little old me,

By the time you read this, you would probably be in Lagos with that man. So, I would like to relay some information to you. I will stuff this letter at the back of the basin in the last hostel you stayed at during your university years. I hope you find this in good health and probably wealth as well.

You remember staring at an aeroplane while he stood there talking to you. You also remember thinking that your paradise can never find you again. Daddy had spoken to his long term friend after Michael but you weren't ready yet. You slept at a friend's house when it happened. At the time, you were back home, going out to Anita's hotel.

You had imagined flowers, maybe red rose petals spread on the bed with a bottle of champagne (probably red wine) and candlestick placed in strategic position that resembles a heart. You recited this in your heart because you probably didn't want to believe it. I wouldn't either.

You might have known the outcome because you took your night things. You took your toothbrush, facial and body skincare products and a flimsy purple nightgown. You convinced yourself that you would spend the night there. It's just for precaution. You placed them in your small purse and you thought, If worse comes to worse, you would lay your body down for him. You convinced yourself that because there is no other option than that.

You and him have never fought. You didn't quarrel with him either but you could sense that something was wrong somewhere. You felt it in your bones. Not only did you feel that something was wrong, you knew that your backup plan won't come to fruition. Laying your body is being pathetic and maybe, it looks like selling it to the devil; but the most important thing you felt is that you just couldn't do it. You couldn't destroy yourself that way.

You arrived that day and just like you suspected, he went all out. He screamed and made a scene just to embarrass you. You were numb and quiet. You already knew the outcome and why it happened. There's nothing like a good eavesdrop. Mummy was sobbing that night when you stomped out of the dinning room but you were able to hear her last statement before you were out of earshot.

What you didn't expect is to see a different girl come up the stairs. She was pretty, you remembered thinking. He called her darling and beckoned on her. He left you there and you remember thinking, your last resort didn't come in handy. Two timing can be a bitch slap in the face at times.

You slept at your friend's but the next day, you met your daddy's choice He's too old, you acknowledged that. Many people would love to marry him of course but you can't marry a man with four wives and many girlfriends. How mummy trained you and what daddy expected gave you the will to go through the introduction.

Apparently, you are only a silverware to everyone. You are needed to an extent but you would be dropped if your mission is done. Michael did the same thing. Father did the same thing and now, mother and this man wants to do the same thing. You couldn't go living your life like that.

You met someone that would help you get amnesia. As a doctor, you know what and how to do it. You want to wake up as a newborn from the womb of a different mother. You want to change your life. If you are reading this, your memory have been jogged. Daddy's choice should not live. He needs to die.

In this letter, there's cyanide in crystalline solid. Chronic cyanide poisoning would seem like a gradual onset of an illness. Headaches can suggest anything. Anxiety can make any mother be frightened for her son. Chest pain can be equivalent to an onset of pneumonia. Remember that you should add miniscule quantity to his meals but never his drink especially water. Live your life the way you want to. Just as he suggested.

PS: He's not to be solely trusted. Make sure he's thrown in prison for what he did.

Your bestie,

A glow in the dark

The ambulance drove quickly. There have been an accident and Joy Chilotam, Dr and Dr. Mrs. Chilotam and Mr. Ezeja were rushed into the emergency unit. Joy needed surgery and Michael is the lead surgeon. Mr. Ezeja died on the spot and both doctors were in critical condition. The man died first but Dr. Mrs. Chilotam struggled to live. Joy was taken in for surgery but the lead surgeon was late.

Before he started his operation even as the heart monitor started beeping and every nurse tried to perform CPR, he stared at her and said,

"It didn't worked."


Far away in Isakaita hostel at Nsukka, a town in Enugu, Nigeria, Chioma was washing her hands in a basin. As she tried to turn off the tap, she bumped the basin with her hip and something fell off. It's ten o'clock in the night and she's the only one at the toilet end. She was curious as she picked it. Inside there was a letter and a paper envelope that had something she suspected to be marijuana. She opened the letter and started reading it. For a while, she was shocked but the familiarity gave her that upturned smile she only reserved for disgusting barmen.

## ONE LOST, A HUNDRED MORE TO GO

Oditanma picked up her brush once more. She was going for one stroke and that's all. This one piece was what she has been working on for a week. The art exhibit is in a week and she couldn't feel more prepared. Her previous works have garnered her recognition and a chance to go abroad. This one would seal the deal. She's been preparing all this while. Her bags were packed and her leash is almost up. She doesn't need to pay for her house that she wouldn't be in need of in the near future.


She was calculating how much money that would remain in the bank. She doesn't intend to spend it. She just wanted to hold on to some cash in case she needed anything. Ebuka stared at her for a while. He's being at the academy for far longer than she and yet, there she is receiving what he's always wanted.

Amaka, their mentor told him to stick with her. He would learn something from her, she said. She's a natural when it comes to this things, she said. And of course, she's the best. Who wouldn't want to stick with the best? He stuck with her, to a point that she got angry with him and he had to timidly apologize to her. She's stuck up, he would admit within himself but in public, he would say that she's bold and self-confident.

He has always envied her. She seemed to have everything under control. She has talent, a house, money; even a car. She rarely drives it though. Her driver sometimes picks her up and sometimes, she takes the bus or a taxi. People in the academy may call it humble, he calls it showoff.

"Odita,..." he called, "Come on. Everyone's packing. Let's go."

Oditanma doesn't like Ebuka. He's like a pest to her. She could sense that he hates her but while he pretends to like her is beyond her. Ever since their mentor, Amaka had given specific orders for him to learn from her, he followed her everywhere. He would compliment her on any slight thing she does. Oh, she wore a pretty blue dress, he would exclaim and scream, telling everyone how pretty her dress looked. Oh, she took Kelvin's offer to take her to the academy and he would call her humble. She hated how over exaggerating he is to her. Even right now, he's giving her a signal like a traffic light as if she didn't know that they are closing.

Everything was ready. All she had to do was wait untill the painting dries. After that, she would put it up for everyone to see. She came outside, onto the balcony. She lived on the fourth stair of an apartment building. She's always preferred upstairs. The view from ups stairs is breathtaking and she would kill for a view like the sunset every evening.

Suddenly, there was a shadow flying towards her. She couldn't make out the object. It seemed like a bird but more sinister, like it had yellow eyes and big sharp claws, probably sharper and bigger than a falcon's. It made a terrible noise as it flew. She didn't mind it at all. This must be a new species of bird. She would paint it or maybe, catch it and tame it. They would be a cash reward to see that.

She waited with a baited breath as it flew towards her. It was fast, very fast and she didn't know how it happened. One moment she was staring at it, marveling at the wonders of nature and the next, she felt it as it scratched her eyes and she couldn't see a thing.

She felt her way around her surroundings, wondering why the moon had to shut off it's light or maybe, NEPA has taken the light. Her chest kept on growing tighter and tighter and she couldn't breathe. But yet, she kept on searching for a source of light, any source of light.

She could hear the neighbors. They were shouting and for some reason, their voices seemed extra high. She felt the handle of a door and opened it like usual, her chest squeezing and growing tighter. She didn't see anything. At that moment, she fell down. The hole was too dark and she couldn't make out anything. She just kept on falling and falling. An eternal fall, a fall from the heavens like those fallen angels on their way to the depths of hell. Nobody held her.

There was no strong hold for her to grab onto. It's just that eternal fall, that everlasting fall that will never end. And she was afraid. Sometimes, she felt like she would hit the floor but it never came. She felt like if she really does hit the floor, it would really hurt and so she thought, it's better to fall without a tangible substance to fall on.

The hole was large and dark like space until it wasn't. At first, it felt like she was floating. That eternal fall that put that fear but still made her hang onto hope suddenly stopped. She is floating. She's in space. Floating put more fear into her. Would she be in limbo her entire life. She was scared. For some reason, floating made her more afraid than falling. Falling means that she could at least dream that she would have a solid landing but floating means that she would cease to exist.

For a while, she struggled and soon, a force threw her with a magnitude that she felt breathless. Then, she could hear them. People calling her and saying something. They were around her, she knew. She could feel them, hear them but she couldn't see them. Being in a state of limbo didn't seem like a bad idea now that she seems reanimated somehow. Everything seemed the same but different. They were intact like she had them but that difference stood out and she knew why now. She's blind.

Everything flew by very quickly. First, it was the academy. She couldn't paint when she was blind and so, they had to revoke her admission. It's for her own good , Ebuka had said to her the day he came to tell her the good news. Oh, he also said that her last painting would be auction since the owner is blind. The money would help her recuperate, as if she can recover from blindness.

Next came her landlord. Her time in the apartment is up and he didn't care if she was blind. Someone has paid for the apartment in full and will soon move in. She's to move out before the week is up. Then, next came who she would call to help her. Her siblings were a pain in the ass. They refused to cater for her. They have families and jobs. They have responsibilities. Their life is far much better than that stupid blind girl's own. Then, next came self-pity. Reminiscing about the past and how awesome she was as a painter. She was talented and the best of the best. Nobody can best her in that field. Not even Leonard de Vinci.

The man is a caricature at best. She remembered the sound of birds and how they looked like. She remembered her neighbor's voice, distinguished them and gave them faces. Mr. Law has a pigeon face but his beak is white in colour. Mrs. Barnabas has an owl face but she's too short that her face can only turn in two directions, 180 degrees. Dr. RM has the face of a turkey but with a purple beak.

As they packed her stuff and her landlord screamed obscene words at her, she still thought about them but this time, her landlord has the face of an ostrich but without a beak. They threw her out of the house and she fell and bruised her arms. The stones were made from thorns because they pinched her no matter how much she tried to get them out.

She sat on her bags in front of the house, she's sure. She could hear the traffic. She could hear the neighbors but nobody spoke to her until one day. She heard her mother's voice. Her mother seemed to be crying. She is thin, her mother said. She looks haggard. She's lost a lot of weight. See how her skin is sagging and her bones are sticking out.

She never wanted to call her mother. Her mother lived in the village. She enjoyed city life. The hustle and bustle of the city, the chatter of the neighbors, the streetlights, that feeling that you are better than everyone else in your respective homes and maybe, the noisy traffic.

The village has none of those and so she preferred to sit on her bag all day than return to the village to build the life she had abandoned a long time ago. Of course, her mother didn't know that. Instead, she threw her into whatever car or lorry she hired and off they went, far away from the big city.

She's miserable. The village was worse than the city. In the city, she could identify sounds and be able to pinpoint what it was but the village was very quiet. There is rarely any noise in or out of the house. At first, she wondered if she was in a graveyard. Every now and then, the village children would scream and giggle and she would say, oh, I left the city for the village.

Her mother never complained and this she hated. She wanted her mother to scream and banter with her on how she got blind and useless. Everyday, she would feel like her eyes were closed to the world and she would be gone for a while. But she would wake up and can never tell the difference between sleep and wakefulness.

Every now and then, her mother would take her for a walk. She would sit under a tree and her mother would talk to her about the village. She never mentioned how she came to have a blind daughter. And for a while, she would feel miserable about what she thought about her mother.

With time, death didn't come as she had anticipated. She decided to get acquainted with her surroundings. She spoke with her mother and they would joke a lot. She's never felt this close to her. She never thought about her painting talents. Time made them a distant memory. She was known and she knew. Everyone said her name but no one knew who she was. She was called one of the greatest painters in the academy but she quit for some unknown reasons.

At first, she was angry. But then, she grew saddened by it and now, she's come to accept it. She taught the village children how to speak English and sometimes, she sings for them. She was made the voice of the village whenever people of importance come to the village. She spoke with them and also sang whenever she was told to. Her voice was known throughout the village and it was of great help. An important figure had her taken back to the city and she became a well-known singer. She decided to look up and not down like her usual self. Of course she's still blind but if she wasn't, she would have been a painter with a narrow-minded attitude.

# A BAD DATE

Living my home to Chitis restaurant on a date is not my ideal way to spend a Sunday afternoon. A friend of mine set me up on a blind date with a professor in our university. She said that he is a little old but I could deal with a little old man. My mind is set on marrying any man that is ready for marriage. I've been single after I hit spinster age which is eighteen for me. For twelve years, no man have ever approached me and I can't help but wonder why. I've been on blind dates since forever but neither of those men called me for a second date nor asked for my phone number. I don't know if I look or sound desperate but this has to stop.

I stood at the entrance of the restaurant and waited for my so called blind date. I caught the eye of a guy who was watching me from his car. He climbed out of the car and headed towards me. I fidgeted on my shoes and bowed my head shyly. I thought about what to say to him.

"Hello..."

"Hi..."

"What is a beautiful girl like you doing standing around here?"

"I'm waiting for my date."

"Your date?...," he said thoughtfully

He stroked his chin which is scarce of beards and said,

"Are you married?"

"No, sir."

"Do you have a boyfriend?"

"No, sir."

"Then, I guess we will get along just fine."


He grinned at me and I smiled. He jutted out his elbow and I took it. He smiled at me and I suppressed my giggle as we made our way into the restaurant. He left me and made to go and order our lunch. He didn't ask me what I would like to eat and I didn't mind. He got himself jellof rice and got for me fried rice.

It's amusing how males seem to think that fried rice is an everyday female meal. I ate my meal delicately as we started a conversation. He talked about himself and what he likes doing but he never commented on his profession when I asked him about it. I talked about myself too but I tried to lessen the way I speak in order not to dominate the conversation. After lunch, he bought me a pub of vanilla ice cream and took me to his car. We drove around campus pointing at places we've been and places we would like to go to.

At approximately 5 o'clock, I told him that I ought to go home but he told me that there is a place he hadn't shown me yet. With that, we left campus and he made a right turn into the road that lead to Oba. We drove without speaking or pointing at anything of interest and the atmosphere automatically turned serious. I was scared but I wanted to trust him. He is the first man to have paid me any attention and I guess he can't harm me.

Can he?

I shrugged inwardly. After all, my friend knows that I am with him. With that, I settled my fears. He turned into an untarred road and drove wildly. I held onto the hanger of the car as we swished and swivelled. He turned into a bushy area and slowed down. He packed his car under a cashew tree and said,

"Wait here."

"What are we doing here?"

He smiled so widely that I thought that his lips will split into two.

"It's a surprise."

"Am I meeting your parents?"

"Sort of."

He grinned cockily and I smiled back nervously. He closed the door and I looked around my surroundings. I don't see any houses nor thatched huts around and I know that he didn't bring me here to dance under the moonlight like those over dramatic Nigerian romantic movies. My phone lit up and I tapped on the message.

"Prof. Ejike said that he wouldn't make it. He said that I should apologize for him and that he would have a make up dinner with you tomorrow."

I looked up from my phone slowly and stared across the driver's sit. In hindsight, I was to be at home, eating macaroni and watching cheesy dramas on African magic. I was supposed to be reading for my test tomorrow on my bed. I was supposed to be grieving my loss of yet another eligible bachelor because he had stood me up.

But here I am, in the middle of nowhere, fearing my demise. It's very clear now, his demeanor and how he treated me. It was all a pretence on his part. I was just a cheap girl in his hands. I sent a quick message to my friend.

"Call the police. Tell them that I'm under the hands of a ritualist."

No sooner have I sent that message, my door opened to three masked men. They drew me by my arms but the belt buckle held me in place. Someone unbuckled me and they carried me to a clearing. They striped me of my clothes except my underwear and for a second, I thought that they would rape me before they kill me but I heard them saying,

"Is the fire ready?"

"Yes."

"And the pot."

"Yes"

"Should we cut the neck first?"

"Poke the skin to see how skinny she is."


Someone pricked my skin with a knife. They drew my hair and started cutting it, hurting my scalp in the process.

"This women and attachment. It usually makes our work harder."

"Next time, don't catch a female with attachment," someone grumbled


They tied my hands and legs, put a tape over my mouth and started flogging me. I would have screamed but I had a tape over my mouth. The torture was too much for me to bear over a simple date. At a point, they stopped flogging me and I heard someone saying,

"She's ready."

Soon, I could feel a blade on my throat cutting through. I struggled to run from the blade but my struggles were weak. I could feel myself losing consciousness. I vaguely felt someone carry me and place me on something hot that stung my skin. The smell of burning skin drifted through the air and into my nose. I didn't have the strength to jerk out. I could feel my strength drain from me. My last thought was, "God, may they receive their due."

## A SURVIVAL

She's currently sitting on one of the benches in the lecture hall trying to listen in on conversations from her classmates. What were they saying? Did they know? Why are they staring at me? Is the lecturer trying to call the police? Why is he gripping his phone like that? Have I gone crazy?

These were the questions that were running through her head. Fear gripped her as she held her pen. It's just another lecture, she told herself. It's just another day. I will get through it, she told herself. But she couldn't even hear the lecturer; with the roaring wind around her and her blood rushing through her ears, blocking the only person she wanted to listen to. She wasn't able to jote down anything. She didn't even know the topic that was discussed.

Why me?

The mad dash of students around her woke her up from her thoughts. The lecturer have left the hall and her classmates were rushing for the next class. Good for them, she thought. They didn't have a complicated life like hers, filled with overrun thoughts swimming through her head like an eel.

She picked up her notebook and her handbag. Hugging her books to her chest and carrying her handbag across her shoulder, she walked along with her bustling classmates. Everyone was talking at the same time; do we have any assignments? What did Dr. Onoha say about so so so and so course. What about your projects? Nobody talked about the incident. It's like the university campus is innocent of that horrid event.

"Chisom!" someone called her.

She turned towards the voice. Chi-Chi, short for Chioma, ran towards her. Her handbag slipped from her shoulder as she tried to keep it up across her shoulder. She tied her braid up in a ponytail but it seemed lose that the updo threatened to spill across her back.

She and Chioma have been friends since first year and they seem to kick it off as soon as they met. They became closer when they found out that they were in the same department. Ever since then, they were attached to the hip. Most people called them twins and they were happy to show off twin gene if anyone called them that. But the day's event have made her want to rethink her relationship with Chioma.

"Hey, Chi-Chi." she said.

"Jeez, Chisom. You've been off since I saw you in class. You didn't even notice me when I called you from the front. I saved you a seat for Christ sake." she shouted, above the noise of students running around the building to get to their next class.

Chisom stared at Chi-Chi for a moment. She would never understand, she thought.

"Am fine," she said, "And am sorry for ignoring you. I didn't see you there."

"What happened to you? You normally don't stay at the back. Are you okay?" Chi-Chi asked.

"I'm okay. I just need some air."


She didn't have the strength to talk and she wanted to communicate with Chi-Chi through her words which Chi-Chi seem to get. She nodded and said,

"You want to sleep it out? I can cover for you."


She shook her head and said,

"I want to attend class today. I will just stick by you for now."

"Alright." Chi-Chi said.


She hooked her arm around Chisom's and said,

"Come on, let's get you to class."


Chisom allowed a small smile to brighten her face and then, they were off. She wasn't dumb when she walked along side Chi-Chi. She knew the news would sooner or later reach her department but she didn't know which one she would want to happen, sooner or later.

The news spilled around campus that evening. Chisom was lying on her bed in the hostel when she heard her roommate screaming. She opened her eyes and peered at her final year roommate. Ada was always a drama queen. She would make unnecessary noise for something as trivial as a half eaten sandwich or maybe, she only dropped her phone.

"What is it?" Olanna asked Ada.

Chisom rolled her eyes. Olanna is not much of a drama queen like Ada but she likes to feast on it like a leech. She would do anything for a drama but that could be likely linked to her studying theater arts.

"Collins is dead." she screamed.

Chisom closed her ears to block out the piercing sound.

"Who is Collins?" Olanna asked.

"Are you crazy? He's in your department; same year, same course and you don't know him?" Ada screamed.

"You mean, Ossai Collins?" Olanna asked.

"Yes!" Ada screamed.

"What?! How?! Where?!" Olanna screamed too.

Chisom was planning on a way to shut this two up until she heard what they said.

"Multiple stab wounds. I have the pic but it's disgusting. He's dick is out too but that got stabbed as well." Ada said.

"You mean, he was masturbating when they stabbed him. Even in death, he still thinks about sex." Olanna laughed.

"I will say ew but his dead. So, we need to pay him our respect." Ada said.

Olanna snorted and said,

"Like he deserves one."

Chisom startled them by saying,

"Can I see the picture?"

"What for?" Ada asked.

"Biological references." Chisom said.

Ada scrunched her face and said,

"Am an undergraduate in pharmacy and I don't see the need to do that."

"Can I please just have the pic?" Chisom said, feeling tired of Ada's childish behavior.

"I will send it to you on WhatsApp. That way, we don't get to squeeze." she said, already typing on her phone.

She received the message due to the wifi that have been on for a few hours. Her breathing stopped immediately she saw the pic. It's something she couldn't wipe from her memory. He was lying in the same place, beside the dustbin located near the faculty of arts building. His trousers were pulled down to reveal a mangled penis. His shirt has dried blood on it and the stab wound on his forehead looked like he bashed it on something instead of a knife wound. His eyes were wide open, still surprised from the attack he took. Chisom couldn't take her eyes away from the picture. She's the one that did all that. She hadn't meant to but if she didn't defend herself, the boy would have taken her virginity. She would rather kill him then be disvirgined.

She stared at Ada as she gushed on who the hero was. Who killed the amazing and famous Ossai Collins? While Olanna cautioned her to be quiet. That person would obviously go to jail, she said. Jennifer, another roommate, ran into the room screaming,

"Did you guys hear the news?"

"Yes, Jenny. Collins is dead." Olanna said.

"I wanted to date him, you know." Jenny said.

"Ew! That boy will use you for his sexual release. Just like that." Ada snapped her fingers to emphasize how fast Collins can use someone.

"I don't care. I heard he's good." Jenny said.

"I would rather go for Dr. Ichie's lectures than get disvirgined by him." Olanna screwed her face.


Ada let out a hollow laugh. What a way to spend an evening, Chisom thought. She felt like drowning in her own blood. Maybe if she died, she wouldn't feel anything anymore. She hid herself behind her wrapper while listening to what her roommates said. Obviously, he has been a sexual addict. She should be happy that she got rid of him for some girls like Olanna. But she didn't feel relieved. Instead, she remembered what transpired between them before the accident happened.


That early morning, only today by five, she was coming back from night class. She always did this. She would have done it with Chi-Chi but she's not a fan of night class. She was scared of the things that could happen to a female student, obviously the stories she's heard about. Looking at it in that perspective, Chi-Chi wasn't wrong. Those stories have visited her as well, in the form of a fair and handsome boy. He attended the night class as well but he, obviously, wasn't there to read. Instead, he was disturbing her while she was reading and she didn't get much things done.

This annoyed her to her core and she packed up and left the hall. She didn't know that the boy followed her. As she passed the faculty of arts building, he showed himself. There was no moon and so, she couldn't see his face clearly. He had said,

"Some girl you are. Can't let a guy get something fresh."

She was scared and her hands were clammy. Her gown stuck to her skin as the wind blew softly. She was shaking. She has heard about rape but she never dreamed it would be done to her as well.

"Now be a good little girl and don't scream. Though, I like the screaming ones." he said, grinning.

"God is watching you." she had said.

What he said struck her to the bones. He has raped girls before. He looked at her and started laughing. He didn't mind that there might be others walking around. He just laughed like that.

"I like the godly ones too." he said.

Chisom prepared to scream but he held her mouth, brandishing a short knife in front of her.

"If you scream, I will stab you. It's just one sex, babe. What more can it give you but a baby. Death will throw you away from the world. Losing your virginity is not special, babe. Just let lose for once."


The tears were coming in a rush. She sniffed, trying to stop it but the boy must have noticed.

"Aw, she's crying. But we've not started yet. I want you to cry when I slam on you."


She didn't say anything. He laid her on the tarred road and struggled with his zipper while holding her legs down.

"It would be over before you know it." he said in a husky voice.


He situated himself in her entrance and she struggled. He laughed at her pathetic attempt but he didn't see her reach for the knife. Next thing she knew, she has stabbed his chest. He fell on top of her but she pushed him away.


Staring at him, she felt a plausible anger run through her. She picked up the knife and stabbed his penis two times, stabbed his forehead two times and stabbed his chest again. When she realised what she has done, she ran away taking the knife with her. She threw it at a gully, knowing fully well that they burn refuse there. She has gotten back in record time, before her roommates got up but she's never been the same ever since.


The next day, she went to school. She heard the murmurs, the insults as her classmates talked about the news. Everyone thought she was a cold blooded murderer. She couldn't take it anymore. She left the classroom and went to Abuja building. The building has always been known as that but in actuality, it's the faculty of physical science building. She stared at everyone on the ground floor, wondering if it would hurt to jump off the top of the building.

"Are you okay?" someone said.

"Yes." she said.

"Why are you putting your foot at the edge of the building?" he asked.

"Life..." she said.

"Everyone has problems." he said.


She laughed.

"Mine is worst." she said.

"Really? Try me." he said.

"I killed someone." she said.

"Did he deserve it?" he asked.


She hesitated before saying,

"Yes."

"If he deserves it, why are you trying to kill yourself?"

"I shouldn't have done that." she said.

"Any valid reason why not?" he asked.


She didn't have anything to say.

"Didn't think so."

"It's just that I think I've gotten my hands dirty."

"Chisom, if you didn't kill him, you would be pregnant now. So, do not blame yourself for men's failure to keep their sexual urges to themselves." he said.


She looked at the males below. They were talking happily, laughing while a female they might have raped will be somewhere out there crying. They would boast to their friends about a quick sexual incident and the females will try to pacify themselves, maybe go through abortion or keep the baby. Suddenly, she felt angry. The guilt she felt for the said Collins Ossai was thrown to the wind. She would live her life to the fullest. She wouldn't let women slavery dictate her life. She is who she is now, a survival.

**A STATE OF UNREST**

I saw it before I felt it. Mum had the case of a brewing fever and so, she retired earlier than us. Dad sat on the cushion in the parlor watching the latest news on NTA channel while Oluchi, the eldest child tried to coerce James to take his night bath. He doesn't like bathing, something to do with stripping and having to take his bath by someone other than himself.

Whenever big sis trys to bath him, he would jump out of the bathtub and run around the house naked, goading sis to run after him. I sat in the balcony with my art supplies trying to replicate the sunset. My dream is to be an artist in the near future but I guess sometimes, dreams are like stars. You are looking at them but you can't reach them.

The unrest began when I heard noises coming from outside our fence. At first, I thought it might be the neighborhood boys smoking as usual behind our fence but I guess I was wrong. I heard three gun shots from below me. It wasn't so near that I could feel it and it wasn't so far either that I couldn't hear it.

I heard someone screaming. I can recognize Oluchi's voice wherever I am. It has this deep timbre resonating from her chest and it sounds masculine. She's proud of it because she thinks her voice can coerce James and I to obey her every wimp as the eldest child.

I dropped my paintbrush and quietly opened the door. The whole house was very quiet and I wondered, for a second, if I only imagined those gun shots but then, I heard unfamiliar masculine voices downstairs and I felt goose bumps spreading throughout my body. Their voices sounds very deep and rough like our neighborhood boys which made me think that they are likely chainsmokers.

Fear gripped me and I tightened my fist around the handle of the door to the balcony. I know that I should be downstairs right about now, I should try to save my family or die trying but someone has to survive this. I didn't have the phone to call the police and even if I did, I don't know the police emergency number. I pressed my palms together as I stared at my painting. I prayed to God that they wouldn't find me. I hoped that they wouldn't find mum and I hope that dad, Oluchi and James were alright. Large tears pooled at the bottom of my eyelid and spilled from my eyes and I couldn't blink them away.

The door opened so suddenly and forcefully that I found myself jumping to the sound. A man dressed in black clothes, a black mask covering every part of his face expect his eyes which had holes around them for easy vision appeared behind the open door. He laughed a funny kind of laughter and shouted to his companion,

"You were right. She's in the balcony."

I stared at him, bewilderedly. I knew my tears were streaming down forcefully but I could do nothing about it.

"You know that you are a coward. Your family are downstairs pleading on your non-existent self and you are here, crying."

Surprisingly, he spoke good English for a criminal. Most criminals that I have seen spoke pidgin English with a specific accent or they spoke their native language. English language seems foreign coming from a criminal's lips to me.

"Come here...," he said, "... We want all of you downstairs."

I stood up from my sit, shakenly and started walking. He used the tip of his gun to hustle me forward making me shudder in fright. As I made my way downstairs, I passed the dinning room and saw how messy it was. Normally, I would worry myself on who would clean the room but right now, that is the least of my worries.

My family laid face down on the floor with their hands on their heads but I felt like there is something missing. As my eyes searched around the sitting room for what was missing, I found what I missed straught on the floor. James' naked body lay immobile on the floor, his mouth open like he had wanted to scream and his eyes looking up at the ceiling. I didn't need the blood pooling around his stiff body or the bullet lodged in his forehead to know that he's dead.

I was numb as I laid on the floor and put my hands on the back of my head. I can hear Oluchi whimpering and mum look like she's passed out on the floor. Dad didn't move neither did he make a sound. The only sign of movement he made is the rise and fall of his body showing that he's still alive but either he's breathing violently or he's trying to control he's breath.

"We are not here for your money...," the robbers said, "We are here for your girls. So, if you would kindly give us your girls, we will set you free."

Nobody said anything. I wanted to look at Oluchi but I don't want to bring any unwanted attention to myself. I've heard about rape, those who are sexually abused but it always seemed like something otherworldly; something that happens to others, something that happens in other places. I never dreamed that it would happen here in our own home.


Oluchi is only sixteen and she's still in senior secondary 2 and I am fourteen. I am to write my NECO exams next week but I doubt this robbers will understand. They would have want to satisfy themselves before any of them would want to know that we still have our lives to live; before they would want to know that Oluchi needs her WACE certificate or she wouldn't write her JAMB examination that will gain her entry into the university.

"Did you hear me?," someone said, addressing us or maybe dad.


My tears were coming in multiple sobs now but I tried to rein it in. Crying outloud will do me no good.

"If you don't do as we say, we will use your mother and after that, we will still force you."


For a moment, I thought dad will oblige to their request for mum's sake but dad didn't say anything. I wondered why everyone chose to remain quiet. I wanted to scream but I couldn't. I didn't want to get raped but I didn't want mum to get raped either. I heard footsteps but I couldn't pinpoint where they were headed.

"She's passed out already? Do you think we should just kill her?," someone said.


I wanted to scream in protest but no sounds could form in my throat. Someone raised my face up and I am eye level with a familiar pair of eyes. I will never forget this eyes. This is Nnamdi, our neighbor's disobedient son. He is in my class but he had repeated Junior secondary 3, JS3 three times. He has asked me on a date once but I turned him down. I didn't know that one little problem will bruise his ego.


He started dragging me towards the guest room. I didn't have the strength to protest but I could hear Oluchi kicking and screaming as Nnamdi dragged me all the way to the guest room. He closed the door behind him and locked it. He approached me slowly and quietly as if stalking a cornered animal. I stared at him without moving an inch and he chuckled,


"You have no idea how much I have wanted you ever since I saw you in grade 5. You were this small...," he lowered his arm to a certain height with his palm facing downward, smirking mischievously, "...but you matured very quickly."

He kept his gun on the ground and started fumbling with his belt buckle.

"I will make this worth your while," he said

I stared at him as he fumbled with his zipper. He was too busy to see me staring at his manhood within his trousers straining to be free. He was too busy stroking himself to see me staring at the gun he kept too close to me. He was too busy to see me reaching out and holding the gun in my tight fist. I guess I was just too numb to think about it. So much have happened in this dreadful night that I didn't mind being thrown into a jail cell. I pulled the trigger at him and before he realise that I had him, I pulled the trigger and shot his manhood.

# THE MUMBLES

He entered the church, quietly. It looked packed to the point of spilling. The church wardens didn't pay him any mind, neither did the male child currently staring at him say anything to him. It was like an open book. He went into the Catholic Church like a man buying something from the market.

He looked around him watching everyone to see if they would notice him but everyone seemed oblivious. He didn't know what he was hoping for, a miracle maybe. Maybe, he wanted the Reverend father to recognize him and point him out. But everyone had their mind on the homily the father was chatting about, not giving him a second glance.

He shook under the pressure of his own fear. He has been standing by the door for more than a minute but still, he couldn't move a muscle. They told him to go to the center of the church. They told him that he would be saved, just like everyone. He has never been to a church before and whatever he had imagined before was far from what he's looking at.

The church is large and is supported by several pillars. It has a high ceiling converging at the center to form an arc. Iridescent saints were plastered on the stained glass windows on the ceiling as well as the windows and doors around the church. And the people attending the church were dressed in expensive clothings. Even the little children running around the church were dressed to the max.

For a moment, he thought their life wouldn't amount to anything if he did it but the guilt he felt threw over the anger, jealousy and disgust. They were still people; they have a family, a job and a life. Why would anyone want to take that away from them. Someone tapped him on the shoulder, gently. He turned to the person and the person, a church warden, he realise, stared back at him.

"Is their any problem, sir?"

He wanted to nod at him. Oh , he so wanted to nod but fear would not let him. Fear that the terrorist will find out that he rattled them out and besides, he didn't want to be the only one dying. If he died alone, his pieces wouldn't be found and he would be another victim of circumstance. He shook his head at the church warden who gave him a small smile.

"Is this your first time?" he asked.

"What?" his voice sounded like a frog with a cough.

They didn't bother to feed him. Two days would go by and they wouldn't feed him. Even if they do, they give him a meal with either excess water or it is too dry. They had tried to feed him for this mission.

"Are you okay, sir?" the church warden asked.

Finally, someone have noticed him. But the church warden stared at him with something akin to concern instead of suspicion. He felt like he had no voice and no one could hear him. Why should he try anyway, he thought. He cleared his throat and said,

"Yes, I'm fine."

The church warden nodded and said,

"Being to church for the first time can be terrifying but don't worry. You will get use to it."

He nodded like he understood what the flat nosed guy was talking about. For all he knew, today would be his last. Every thought he had while they got him here, how he had planned to rat them out and save millions of people had vanished. Not that his fear was too overwhelming but his anger and maybe jealousy for the expensive clothings the church goers spend their time on was enough to feed his family of four.

He had been a normal husband, a normal son and a normal father. His sons looked up to him, his wife adored him and his parents were proud of him. He was the proud worshiper of the almighty Allah, recited the Koran daily and prayed at the right time. He had promised his wife that he wouldn't marry another woman but then, how can he when he doesn't have enough money to feed the hungry mouths he presently have.

He had a shop that sold watches and he repaired most as well. His customers know him by the name, Musa even if he goes by the name, Ahmed Ali. His life was a definition of perfect, well, until a group of terrorist attacked their market. He was taken away like a slave and placed in an underground room that smelled of decayed faeces and overstayed urine. He was the only prisoner and only because he decided to be stupid and hide behind a shelf in his shop. He didn't try to lock the window facing him but then, he didn't notice it until it was too late.

He had stayed there until yesterday. They had brought him out, paraded around him, quoting the Koran and telling him the wondrous things the almighty Allah would grant him if he does the right thing. They planted the bombs all over his body setting it in a way that it would explode if he tries to remove it and they could explode it as well from their camp.

They gave him civilian clothes and told him to act normal. He was too thin due to lack of adequate food but they didn't mind. They only cared about the mission and not the person they are ordering to blast a church. "The church should not be in existence", they had told him, "Mohammed says that we should kill all those who do not worship the almighty Allah." He knew what the Koran said and even if it did say such things, the terrorist had the wrong interpretation of the Koran.

"Were you a Muslim before you got baptized into the Catholic Church?" the church warden asked him, interrupting his wild thoughts.

"Yes." he replied.

The warden smiled and said,

"Come. I will show you a bench."

"No. I will find one myself." I said.

The warden looked annoyed and he narrowed his eyes while saying,

"Suit yourself."

The warden left the entrance of the church while he stood staring at the stained glass windows. He turned towards the church quietly and walked towards the center of the church slowly. He scanned the aisles for a free bench but everyone of them seemed occupied. Every person he passed stared at him like he was crazy. After a while, he gave up and decided to sit on the floor. The woman beside him cleared her throat awkwardly and glanced away from him. People, around him, seemed to be shifting awkwardly on their benches but the homily dragged on.

The church went on and he found himself dreading what is to come. He imagined the Reverend father blowing into bits of tiny human pieces, everyone blowing up and their expensive clothing catching fire, burning away millions and billions of paper money. He pictured what would become of the clothing in his mind. His body didn't give in to laughter like he wanted. Instead, it dragged a bit of fresh air into it's nose to quench the growing anxiety blowing up at the bottom of his tommy.

Why haven't they blown him up yet?

The homily passed and the rest of the church activities continued. He didn't understand any of them. He knew the homily from a customer of his who kept on repeating the word and it's meaning that the word got stuck to his mind, never to get out. He's always thought that churches were noisy but unlike other churches, this catholic church is unusually quiet.

The more they wasted time, the more his anxiety and fear grew. Until finally, he couldn't take it anymore. Everyone were on their feet, shaking hands and hugging each other while whispering whatever into each other's ears. He got up from the ground and ran to the altar; running pass the altar boys that tried to grab him. He grabbed the Reverend father's clothing, which didn't look expensive, he noted and pleaded,

"It's not my fault. Please, do something."


The Reverend father looked terrified staring at the mad man that rushed all the way to the altar only to hold onto his garments.

"Young man," the priest said, "What can I do for you?"

"You can't do anything now. They are coming." the man said, his bloodshot eyes were wide.

"Calm down. I will attend to you after mass." the priest said.

"No!" he screamed


From the corner of his eyes, he saw the church warden that had spoken to him. He wasn't wearing expensive clothes like the church members.

"I'm sorry, father. I didn't know that he is a mad man." he said.

"I'm not mad." the man gestured around.

"Apparently, which explains why you are screaming during mass." the church warden spat at him.

"There are terrorist out to get all of you." he said, gesturing towards the crowded church.

A lot of people screamed while some stared at him, accusingly.

"And how did you know that?" the priest asked

"I know because I was captured by them." he is starting to think that this was not a good idea.

The crowd was in a frenzy, shouting curse words at him and saying that he will not live until the terrorists killed him.

"How did you escape?" the priest asked.

He stared at the priest, trying to gauge what the priest is feeling. He seemed genuinely curious but he couldn't be sure. He shrugged and said,

"I didn't."

"But you said..." the Reverend father tried to say but was interrupted.

"I was captured, yes but my mission is to be a self destructing machine to this church. I have bombs strapped all over my body and if you don't get out, I'll blow up and you will die."

At that, the whole church grew very quiet. No one said a word.

"They have not pulled the trigger yet but if they do, I will self destruct and take this church with me."


The church warden had a terrified look on his face. He was the first person to retraced his steps backwards, quietly turn and run out of the church. His actions triggered the participants in the church because everyone started running. No one payed him any mind. Not even the Reverend father who has already ran off leaving him to deal with his problems. He was the only one who didn't run. A minute now, he would hear the click and he would blow up and he wouldn't remember ever thinking before he died.

**WHAT A FOOLISH MAN**

Killing my dog didn't give me the satisfaction I wanted but selling it did. I don't know what got into the buyer but he bought my dog for sixty million naira worth of cash.

I am rich!

It sang in my mind as I got back to my dilapidated home, only it wouldn't be dilapidated any longer. I bought the land I have been eyeing for a hundred thousand naira and started to grow crops on it. It grew faster than I could ever imagine and I sold them. I earned more than a million naira. I hoped that I would keep on living in millions like I am living now.

I pulled down my dilapidated house and built a mansion. It had two gates, a long driveway and extra security to access the main building. Flowers was an added decoration to the large compound completed with security men holding big black guns and large fierce German Shepherd dogs with their tongues hanging from their mouths, spilling saliva to alert whoever of what their future with the feral dogs entails.

I have twelve cars and three Jeeps parked in an underground garage. I had eight boys at my disposal who would always wash the cars even when I am not using them. I looked at what I have accomplished and smiled but I didn't feel satisfied. Something is wrong somewhere. I think I need an impressive job. I built a company that exports agricultural produce from my home country to anywhere in the world. I import goods as well but that is minimal. This increased my worth to a billion nairas but I wasn't satisfied.

I decided to look for a wife. My first wife is from the Yoruba tribe. She's very pretty and she has a beautiful voice that distinctly emphasis her accent. I would have loved her but her meal is quite the problem. There is never a meal she prepares without a large quantity of pepper added to it. I am relatively tired of it and I want someone who would prepare a meal I can eat.

My second wife is of the Hausa tribe. She's very shy in things she needn't be shy with. She takes her Muslim responsibilities very seriously. Even after we got married, she refused to remove her hijab in front of me, something about me converting from my religion before she would sacrifice herself. I am so frustrated by that attitude and so, I decided to take in another wife.

My third wife is of the Igbo tribe. She's very sensitive and rarely cooks especially when it seems like I angered her. She loves to gossip with her friends when they came along which is everyday. My family and business are not save with her and I try to distance myself away from her.

I married twelve more wives but they seem to have one problem or another. I decided against getting married to any more wives and besides, though they have their problems, each one complements the other. Marrying all those women didn't give me the satisfaction I crave. And so, I resulted to sleeping with different women who weren't my wives.

None of them were going to live with me but unlike my wives, they would do anything to please me. I was happy with that aspect but I wasn't satisfied. I laid on my bed surrounded with six women trying to please me and thought about what to do to gain that immense satisfaction I seem to be searching for. Why couldn't I be satisfied with all my accomplishment, I asked myself.

One of the women started tickling my armpit. I tried to surpress the laughter trying to bubble it's way into my mouth but I couldn't. I laughed so hard that I couldn't recognize the immediate silence around me. Soon, I felt something licking my face. It really annoyed me and I tried to shove it away but it didn't go away. Oh my God, who is interrupting my daydream.

I opened my eyes to a dilapidated house, the striking sun hitting my eyes through the cracked ceiling. I could easily pinpoint the pains at my back made by the horrible nights of sleeping on a mat on the cold, hard floor. The assault on my face continued and I know it's no other than my suppose dead dog licking his share of the grub on my face left by the flies.

I blinked my eyes and turned away from the sight that befell me as soon as I woke up. I felt a huge blow in my heart but I refuse to believe it. I am rich, I said to myself. It's better that I believe it than let it cease to exist. I decided to go to one of my best friend's house and tell him what God had done for me. On getting there, my friend greeted me and got me kolanut -- a tradition passed down by our forefathers whenever there's a visitor in one's home. He blessed it and broke it and we chewed the kolanut in silence.

"My friend...," I broke the silence, "... I'm here to tell you that I would love to contest for this year's governorship election."

"What?!" my friend stared at me in disbelief.

"Yes, I am. Did you know that I have gotten so rich that am able to marry fifteen wives, live in a mansion with high security and still aquire twenty concubines like all those rich politicians."

My friend eyed me with trepidation.

"My friend...," he said, "...are you sure?"

Is he doubting me, I asked myself.

"Of course, it's true. I will show you."

"What happened that made you think that you are rich?," he asked

"I killed my dog and someone bought it for sixty million naira. I am freaking rich."


My friend was alarmed. I don't blame him. I couldn't believe it myself when I saw it. He screamed,

"Chai!! But that dog is your ticket to trick people that you are blind."

"I know but I killed it."

"Are you sure?"

"Come, let me show you."


He looked at me, doubtfully and nodded.

"I will reserve my comments for now. Let me see that sixty million."


I took him back to my house. I was smiling all the way, praying to God for his grace. I don't know what I was expecting but I still trudged on, walking confidently unlike my friend's sluggish walk. We reached my dilapidated house and my dog came out to greet me. I ignored him and rushed into my house. My friend followed me into the wretched home as well.

"Oya...," he said, mockingly, "... show me the money."

I looked around with trepidation and said,

"Wait, let me go back to sleep and get the money."